The World Around Us

Edited by Rob Harding

This book sounds great!

First published in Great Britain in 2016 by:

 Young**Writers**

Remus House
Coltsfoot Drive
Peterborough
PE2 9BF
Telephone: 01733 890066
Website: www.youngwriters.co.uk

All Rights Reserved
Book Design by Spencer Hart
© Copyright Contributors 2015
SB ISBN 978-1-78443-985-9

Printed and bound in the UK by BookPrintingUK
Website: www.bookprintinguk.com

Foreword

Dear Reader,

Welcome to this book packed full of sights
and smells, sounds and tastes!

Young Writers' Sense Poetry competition was specifically
designed for Key Stage 1 children as a fun introduction to poetry
and as a way to think about their senses: what the little poets
can see, taste, smell, touch and hear in the world around them.
From this starting point, the poems could be as simple or as
elaborate as the writer wanted, using imagination and descriptive
language to conjure a complex image of the subject of their
writing, rather than concentrating just on what it looks like.

Given the young age of the entrants, we have tried to include
as many poems as possible. Here at Young Writers, we believe
that seeing their work in print will inspire a love of reading and
writing and give these young poets the confidence to develop their
skills in the future. Poetry is a wonderful way to introduce young
children to the idea of rhyme and rhythm and helps learning and
development of communication, language and literacy skills.

These young poets have used their creative writing abilities,
sentence structure skills, thoughtful vocabulary and, most
importantly, their imaginations to make their poems come
alive. I hope you enjoy reading them as much as we have.

Jenni Bannister

Editorial Manager

Looks like
you're in for a
treat!

Contents

Ampfield CE Primary School, Romsey

Louella Tuffin (5) 1
Charlotte Croxford (6) 1
Beulah Fidler (5) 2
Frankie Pinhorne (6) 2
Archie Wichlacz (6) 3
Mia Windebank (6) 3
Ffion Foster (6) 4
Scarlett Fox (5) 4

Anstruther Primary School, Anstruther

Finch Harris Geary (6) 5
Kyle Wilson (6) 5
Esme Wright (7) 6
Lewis Webster (6) 6
Arran Ogilvie (6) 7
Bradley Finch (6) 7
Charlotte Stewart (6) 8
Kai Guest (6) 8
Alana Munro (6) 9
Reuben Scott (6) 9

Beechlawn School, Hillsborough

Curtis Morris 10
Joshua Gallagher (12) 10
Olivia Cassidy (11) 11
Leah Savage (11) 11
Imogen Watson (11) 12
Corrina Audley (11) 12
Abbey Bickett (12) 13
Carson Rodgers (12) 13

Boskenwyn Community Primary School, Helston

River Beau Markland (6) 14
Henry Cook (6) 14
Felix Currell (5) 14
James Braines (7) 15

Emma Worth (6) 15
Alfred Worth (7) 15
Nathan Roberts (6) 16

Brynteg County Primary School, Wrexham

Carson Scott Jeffrey (6) 16
CJ Richardson (6) 16
Estera Brudel (6) 17
Lily May Borgerson (6) 17
Lee Williams (6) 17
Ioan Prile (6) 18

Crossways Infant School, Bristol

Solomon Compton (6) 18
Evie Smithson (6) 19
Harvey Balding (7) 19
Megan Wareing (6) 20
Eleanor Grace Wickett (7) 20
Amilee Monks (6) 21
Sofiya Perrigo (6) 21
Lucas Jones (6) 22
Sophie Swanston (6) 22
Holly Watson (6) 22
Sophie Clifton (7) 23

Falconer's Hill Infant School, Daventry

Sycamore Class (5) 23
Chestnut Class (5) 23
Maple Class 24
Ash Class 24
Willow Class (7) 25
Oak Class (7) 25

Fishermoss School, Aberdeen

Aimee Thomson (7) 26
Eryn Forbes (7) 26
Owen Willox (7) 26

Fynn Matthew (7).................................. 27
Daniel Wilkins (7)................................. 27
Corey Stephen (7) 27
Emma Jane Marshall (7) 28
Al Rizopoulos (7) 28
Euan Mitchell (7)................................... 28
Arran Cameron (7)................................ 29
Aaron Burns (6) 29
Eilidh Mitchell (7) 29
Isabella Duncan (7) 30
Ahmet Keshiyev (7) 30
Aaliyah Smith (7) 30
Amy Walker (6)...................................... 31
Jay Thompson (7).................................. 31

Glenbervie School, Stonehaven

Callum McInnes (7) 31
Connor Jarvie (7)................................. 32
Amy McPherson (6)............................. 32
Jake Owen (7) 32
Hannah Miller (7)................................. 33
Stuart Jamieson (7) 33

Hambleton CE Primary School, Selby

Danny Hall (6)....................................... 33
Izzy Summerton (6) 34
Seth Harvey (6) 34
Jessica Glover (6)................................. 35
Sophie Bright (6)................................... 35
Tia Hardy (6)... 36
Freya Ruddock (6) 36
Erin McMichan (6) 36

Holy Family Primary School, Londonderry

Caleb Quinn (6) 37
Jake Henry (6)....................................... 37
Riain Barr (6) 37
Lucie-Rose Crossan (7)........................ 38

Holy Trinity CE Primary & Nursery School, Richmond

Dawid Lutynski (6)................................ 38
Emma Lidblom (6) 38

Costya Simonov (6)............................... 39
Madeleine Skager (6) 39
Willem De Haan (6) 39
Kamran Shaha (6) 40
Sam Badawi (6)..................................... 40
Tanvi Mishra (6).................................... 40
Harriet Askham (6)................................ 41
Olivia Moher (6).................................... 41
Caleb Connor (6)................................... 41
Matin MacDermott (7)........................... 42
Zoe Lennon (7)...................................... 42
William Cohn (7).................................... 42
Kennosuke Ken Maeda (7).................... 43
Sonny Matthews (6)............................... 43
Lili Eszenyi (6) 43
Caden Behr (6)...................................... 44
Elliot Jardine (6).................................... 44
Beth Anderson (6)................................. 44
Oscar Allbut (7)..................................... 45
Maximilian Lennox Klos Dias (6) 45
Alexander Pooley (6)............................. 45
Layla Geisler (6)................................... 46
Jonah Neal (6)....................................... 46

Horizon Primary Academy, Swanley

Vincent Window-Beardon (5)................ 46
Liam Chick (5) 47
Harvey Michael Evans (5) 47
Amy Harbour-Chilcott (5)...................... 47
Henry Tapson (5)................................... 48
Roxanne Parker (5)............................... 48
Ayomide Osibona (5)............................. 48
Lexi Kennard (5).................................... 49

Iron Acton CE Primary School, Bristol

Ryan Todd (5).. 49
Rosie Webber (5) 49
Owen McPartland (5)............................. 50
Theo Foote (5)....................................... 50
Ruben Hunt (6)...................................... 50
Katrina Roberts (5) 51

Lainshaw Primary School, Kilmarnock

Lucinda McLeod 51
Capree Jovanna Powell (8) 51
Marni McPherson (8)............................ 52
MacKenzie King.................................... 52
Jessica Dougall 52
Paul Wilkie... 53
Zoe Templeton...................................... 53
Rohan Harkins....................................... 53
Millie Gebbie.. 54
Alexa MacTaggart................................. 54
Heather Mary McAllister (8)................. 54
Brodie Wilson 55
Peter Niven (7) 55
Keira McNelis (8).................................. 55
Allan Brodie 56
Cassie Rooney 56

Pontefract Orchard Head Junior And Infant School, Pontefract

Leo Norbury (5) 56
Sienna Sinclair (5) 57
Tyler Stephen Dillon Montgomery (5)... 57
Joshua Pearce (5) 57
Ethan Smith (5)..................................... 58
Millie G (5) 58
Millen Jay Deravairere (5) 58
Maisie Gregson (5)................................ 59
Edward Raw (5)..................................... 59
Olivia Jane Watton (5) 59
Kian Mark Maundrill (5) 60
Maria Rodzierwicz (5)........................... 60
Lisa Krasauskas (5)............................... 60
Callum Cartwright (6)............................ 61
Layla-Jaimes Carson (6) 61
Jasmine Harrison (5) 61
Frayah Blackburn (5)............................. 62
Liam Joseph William Holdsworth (5).... 62
Cambell Hunton (6) 62
M B (5).. 63

Harry Shaw (6) 63
Alfie Widdowson (5).............................. 63
William James Croft (5) 63

Palmers Cross Primary School, Wolverhampton

Zara Upton (6)....................................... 64
Tianna Esther Sterling (6)...................... 64
Serayah Llewellyn-Brown (6)................. 64
Misbah Chowdhury (7) 65
Mia Alex Sandhu (6) 65
Kairo Williams (6) 65
Liam Beaumont-Pilgrim (6)................... 66
Daniel-Lee Cund (6) 66

Redwood Primary School, Derby

Ajai Tanue (6) 66
Tanvi Parigi (6)...................................... 67
Dylan Holland (6)................................... 67
Kan Adekunle (6)................................... 67
Lily Boyden (6)....................................... 68
Chaise Hackney (6)................................ 68
Joseph Smith (6) 68
Amayah Javed (6) 69
Stefan Chanev (6) 69
Urminder Dhillon (6) 69
Priya Thandi (7)..................................... 70
Zylah Browne (6) 70
Pavandeep Chungh (6) 70
Tom Adelkunle (6).................................. 71
Leila Mae Elliott (6)............................... 71

St James' CE Primary School, St. Helens

Mason Bowles (5).................................. 71
Ben Conway-Henthorn (5)...................... 72
Olivia-Mai Davies (5) 72
Belle Jackson (5) 73
Thomas Mason (6) 73
Ryan Miller (5) 74
Jack Prescott (5).................................... 74
Jorden James Sarbutts (5) 75

Natalie Shannon (6)............................ **75**
Katie Shereen Tabern (5) **76**
Ruby Warner-Southworth (6)............... **76**

St John Ogilvie Primary School, Paisley

Orla Callaghan (5) **77**
Tyler Bourke (6)................................. **77**
Skye McGuire (5)................................ **78**
Freya Martin (5)................................. **78**
Emma Lynch (5) **79**
Rory Price (5) **79**
Jack Gibali (6).................................... **80**
Sean Chitsaka (6)............................... **80**
Harris Hunter (6)................................ **81**
Maria McIntyre (6).............................. **81**
Ava Proctor (6) **82**
Lukasz Lausz (6) **82**
Julian Scott (6)................................... **83**
Daisy Jones (5)................................... **83**
Emily Beattie (6) **84**
Alexander Perry (6) **84**
Charlotte Rush (5) **85**
Louis Wake (6) **85**
Ava Lina Smith (5).............................. **86**

St Patrick's Primary School, Portrush

Amelia Michalska (7) **86**
Thomas Boorman (7)........................... **87**
Beatrice Byrne (7).............................. **87**
Jessica Quinn (7)................................ **88**
Logan Mullan (7)................................ **88**
John Mitchell (7)................................. **89**
Jude Dallat (8) **89**
Tierna Smith (8)................................. **90**
Rory Dillon (7).................................... **90**
Luca McGowan (7)............................... **91**
Dylan Williams (7).............................. **91**
Jaidan Patterson (7) **92**
Kyla Megan Hassan (6)........................ **92**
Charlie Shaw (7)................................. **93**
Eoin John Duggan (7).......................... **93**

St Paul's RC Primary School, Portsmouth

Matthew Inije (7)................................ **94**
Samuel Elms (7)................................. **94**
Neema Saji (6).................................... **95**
Jimnah George (6)............................... **95**

South Hill Primary School, Hemel Hempstead

Patrick Carsey (6)............................... **96**
Jamie Benjamin Wells (5)..................... **96**
Oliver Davies-Moon (5)........................ **97**
Finley Talbot (5)................................. **97**
Ryan Blake Schofield (5)...................... **98**
Isla Stobie (5) **98**
Aaima Ayesha Islam (5)....................... **99**
Joely Burrows (5)................................ **99**
Brooke Barnes (5) **100**
Caelan Jacob Bruce (5)........................**100**
Tanya Knight (5) **101**
Hudson Harte (6)................................**101**
Callum Jell (6)....................................**102**
Ashlee Nicole Jones (6)........................**102**
Japneet Singh (5) **103**
James Dawes (6).................................**103**
Ronnie Tilson (6) **104**
Freya Allford (5).................................**104**
Sophie Harrington (5) **105**
Zara Nield (5).....................................**105**
Rory Stewart (5) **106**
Kiena McFarlane (6).............................**106**

The Cobbs Infant School, Warrington

Emma Brookes (6)...............................**107**
Bella May Ratcliffe (6) **107**

Woodlands Primary School, Borehamwood

Mia Warren (6)...................................**108**
Joel Barrass (6)...................................**108**
Youlin Huang (6).................................**109**

The Poems

Get your nose in this book!

I've got a taste for some poetry!

My Favourite Food

I love the taste of bright red strawberries for my dinner.
I love the sound of crunching cookies in my mouth.
I love the feel of smooth, green apples when I'm having tea.
I love the smell of the cooking chocolate cake in Mummy's kitchen.
I love the sight of the waving apple tree.

Louella Tuffin (5)
Ampfield CE Primary School, Romsey

My Favourite Food

I love the taste of tasty, sweet strawberry in my mouth.
I love the smell of nice, sweet pears.
I love the sight of creamy ice cream in an ice cream cone.
I love the feel of soft, tasty pancakes with some chocolate sauce all over my tongue.
I love the sound of colourful, bubbling pizza in the oven.

Charlotte Croxford (6)
Ampfield CE Primary School, Romsey

What senses did you enjoy reading about on these pages? Colour the symbols.

My Favourite Food

I love the smell of warm, dry, chocolate cookies.
I love the touch of a crunchy apple.
I love cheese pizza warming in my mouth.
I love gammon sizzling under the grill.

Beulah Fidler (5)
Ampfield CE Primary School, Romsey

My Favourite Food

I love the taste of chocolate and vanilla 'Jurassic World' cake.
I love the sound of squishy water coming out of a watermelon.
I love the feel of chocolate ice cream when I lick the cone.
I love dipping my fish fingers in custard!

Frankie Pinhorne (6)
Ampfield CE Primary School, Romsey

What senses did you enjoy reading about on these pages? Colour the symbols.

My Favourite Food

I love the taste of boiling hot chicken in my tummy.
I love the smell of silky, gooey toffee when I open a jar of sweets.
I love the sight of spaghetti Bolognese that Mummy cooks for tea.
I love the sound of crunchy garlic bread that I eat with Domino's pizza.

Archie Wichlacz (6)
Ampfield CE Primary School, Romsey

My Favourite Food

I love the taste of hard-boiled eggs warming up my mouth.
I like the sound of popping candy exploding in my mouth.
I like the sight of melting chocolate making my fingers sticky.
I like the feel of smooth, brown, sausages on my tongue.
I like the smell of pepperoni pizza warming up my mouth.

Mia Windebank (6)
Ampfield CE Primary School, Romsey

What senses did you enjoy reading about on these pages? Colour the symbols.

My Favourite Food

I love the taste of cheesy and nice, warm pizza warming up my mouth, going into my tummy.
I love the sound of crispy and chewy bacon sizzling in the pan.
I love the feeling of hard, cold and yummy chocolate melting in my hand.
I love the sight of brown, squishy sausages sitting on my plate.
I love the smell of the cheesy top on lasagne when it bubbles in the pot.

Ffion Foster (6)
Ampfield CE Primary School, Romsey

Food Senses

I love the taste of juicy, red strawberries.
I love the smell of fruity, green grapes.
I love the sound of spitting sausages.

Scarlett Fox (5)
Ampfield CE Primary School, Romsey

What senses did you enjoy reading about on these pages? Colour the symbols.

Autumn

I can smell a smoky bonfire.
I'm listening to the fireworks zooming fast and high into the sky.
I can see a hedgehog hibernating under a pile of colourful leaves.
I can feel myself snuggling under my smooth, cosy blanket.
I can taste hot chocolate going down my throat and a toasted marshmallow afterwards.

Finch Harris Geary (6)
Anstruther Primary School, Anstruther

Autumn

I can see red, orange and brown leaves and exploding fireworks.
I can hear a crackling bonfire and zooming fireworks that go boom.
I can smell smoke from a lit bonfire.
I can touch a warm, soft blanket.
I can taste hot milk going down my throat.

Kyle Wilson (6)
Anstruther Primary School, Anstruther

What senses did you enjoy reading about on these pages? Colour the symbols.

Autumn

In autumn I see hedgehogs rolling in the leaves and pumpkins in the windows of some houses.
Sometimes you can hear fireworks zooming and crackling high in the sky.
I can smell bonfire smoke in the air.
Autumn tastes of hot chocolate and hot milk.
In autumn you can touch spiky and crunchy leaves and acorns which are smooth and shiny brown.

Esme Wright (7)
Anstruther Primary School, Anstruther

Autumn

I see an orange pumpkin with creepy eyes.
I can hear fireworks zooming fast into the sky.
I smell the hot tomato soup.
I hear crunchy leaves falling from the trees, changing colours on the ground.
I taste hot chocolate, nice and warm in my tummy.

Lewis Webster (6)
Anstruther Primary School, Anstruther

What senses did you enjoy reading about on these pages? Colour the symbols.

6

Autumn

In autumn I see the goldish-brown leaves.
I hear leaves going crunch and fireworks going boom.
I smell smoke coming from a blazing bonfire.
It feels cold outside at spooky and creepy Halloween.
When I go in, I taste hot chocolate and sweets.

Arran Ogilvie (6)
Anstruther Primary School, Anstruther

Autumn

I can see red and orange leaves falling off the tree.
I can hear the fireworks going boom and crackle.
I touch crunching leaves with my woolly gloves on.
I taste the steaming hot chocolate in my favourite mug.
I can smell the smoke from the fireworks zooming in the sky.

Bradley Finch (6)
Anstruther Primary School, Anstruther

What senses did you enjoy reading about on these pages? Colour the symbols.

Autumn

When leaves fall down, I can see red, gold and orange.
When fire pops, I can hear it crackle and sizzle.
When I go to look for leaves, some are spiky when I touch them
and some are not.
When I go to bonfires, I smell fireworks and smoke.
When I am at bonfires, I taste hot milk and toasted marshmallows.

Charlotte Stewart (6)
Anstruther Primary School, Anstruther

Autumn

I can see the exploding fireworks zooming into the sky.
I can hear the leaves crunch when I run.
When I light the bonfire, I smell the smoke.
I like to taste hot chocolate when it is cold.
When I lift the leaves they feel smooth and hard and spiky too.

Kai Guest (6)
Anstruther Primary School, Anstruther

What senses did you enjoy reading about on these pages? Colour the symbols.

Autumn

I can see the colourful leaves falling off the tree.
I can hear the exploding fireworks boom in the sky.
I can smell the smoke-blazing bonfire.
I can touch my blanket, warm, soft and cosy.
I can taste my brown, warm hot chocolate.

Alana Munro (6)
Anstruther Primary School, Anstruther

Autumn

In the woods I see gold and red leaves on the ground.
I can hear fireworks banging and booming up in the dark sky.
I can smell the smoke from the blazing bonfire.
On the ground I can feel the acorns and conkers crackling under my feet.
Autumn tastes like fizzy sweets.

Reuben Scott (6)
Anstruther Primary School, Anstruther

What senses did you enjoy reading about on these pages? Colour the symbols.

Autumn Poem

One scary, dark night, a creaking old door,
Candles flickering in the wind,
Ghost gliding across the floor,
Broken windows, broken graves,
Glowing pumpkins,
Fireworks fizzing,
Scary costumes,
This is Halloween.

Curtis Morris
Beechlawn School, Hillsborough

Autumn Poem

Autumn is my favourite time, I love to trick or treat,
Sweets, toffee apples, apple pie,
The things I like to eat.
Firework displays are really good fun,
Whistling, crackling bright in the sky,
Children cheering, dogs hiding,
Chinese lanterns rising high.

Joshua Gallagher (12)
Beechlawn School, Hillsborough

What senses did you enjoy reading about on these pages? Colour the symbols.

Autumn Poem

In autumn the squirrels sleep through the cold,
Leaves fall from the trees red, yellow and gold,
The clothes you wear keep you cosy and warm,
Blackberries start growing, farmers harvest corn.
You smell the food burning on the stove,
You see the bonfires glowing bright,
Trick or treat can give a fright,
Knocking doors in the dead of night,
Carved out pumpkins burning bright,
This is autumn.

Olivia Cassidy (11)
Beechlawn School, Hillsborough

Autumn Poem

On one scary night, leaves fall off the tree,
Bats go past, frightening me,
Children knocking on the door saying,
'Trick or treat, may I have some more?'
Fireworks burning, shimmering brightly,
Scary noises are very frightening,
Glowing lanterns blowing in the night,
The dark, drizzly, foggy night the animals hibernate,
The wind blows, ghosts come out from the haunted house,
The skeletons awaking in the graves,
Crackling,
Autumn is my favourite season.

Leah Savage (11)
Beechlawn School, Hillsborough

What senses did you enjoy reading about on these pages? Colour the symbols.

Autumn

Trick or treat, smell my feet, give me something nice to eat,
Can I have some candy please?
Walking along on crackling leaves,
I can hear the fireworks whistling,
Children running, excited and screaming,
Knocking doors and glowing pumpkins,
Scary masks and ghostly costumes.

Imogen Watson (11)
Beechlawn School, Hillsborough

Autumn Poem

Scary pumpkins glowing at night,
Skeletons giving us a fright,
Wolves howling, vampires screaming,
Ghosts in the graveyard dreaming,
At school the lights are dark,
Animals hibernate in the park,
Fireworks crackle overhead,
I am cosy in my bed,
But is that a monster I hear?

Corrina Audley (11)
Beechlawn School, Hillsborough

Congratulations your poem has been chosen as the best in this book!

What senses did you enjoy reading about on these pages? Colour the symbols.

Autumn Poem

Howling ghosts, glowing pumpkins,
Leaves squelching, trick or treating,
Eating sweets and toffee apples,
Fireworks booming in the sky,
Autumn is a treat for my senses.

Abbey Bickett (12)
Beechlawn School, Hillsborough

An Autumn Poem

Halloween - the ghost's worst day
The fear of them scares kids away
Ghosts went to be seen as friendly
The strong smell of pumpkins
And the loud bangs of fireworks
The ghosts would rather not come out.

Carson Rodgers (12)
Beechlawn School, Hillsborough

What senses did you enjoy reading about on these pages? Colour the symbols.

Halloween

Halloween feels like monsters eating brains
Halloween smells like death
Halloween tastes like nothing
Halloween sounds like evil graves
Halloween looks like danger.

River Beau Markland (6)
Boskenwyn Community Primary School, Helston

Untitled

Water splashing
Picnics are yummy
The sand is tickly
The flowers smell like sausages
I can see the golden fish.

Henry Cook (6)
Boskenwyn Community Primary School, Helston

Carrots

Carrots sound all crunchy when you eat.
Carrots feel as smooth as silk.
Carrots smell like mucky mud.
Carrots taste of grass.
Carrots look like sunlight.

Felix Currell (5)
Boskenwyn Community Primary School, Helston

What senses did you enjoy reading about on these pages? Colour the symbols.

Halloween

Halloween smells like sweets.
Halloween tastes like fizzy pop.
Halloween sounds like fireworks exploding.
Halloween looks like it's full of ghosts.
Halloween feels like zombies eating my brains.

James Braines (7)
Boskenwyn Community Primary School, Helston

Sadness

Sadness feels like everything around me is rotting.
Sadness smells like rotting food that no one wants to eat.
Sadness tastes like brown and yellow grass.
Sadness looks like everyone is turning their back against you.
Sadness sounds like when you're feeling lonely and you hear nothing.

Emma Worth (6)
Boskenwyn Community Primary School, Helston

Halloween

Halloween smells like stinky slime from a vampire's teeth.
Halloween looks like a dead world, 100 years ago.
Halloween sounds like the whooshing wind of the biggest ghost.
Halloween feels like a whizzing bite of a zombie through my blood.
Halloween tastes like a witch's potion in my mouth.

Alfred Worth (7)
Boskenwyn Community Primary School, Helston

What senses did you enjoy reading about on these pages? Colour the symbols.

Untitled

Happiness sounds like my favourite songs.
Happiness feels like a soft butterfly.
Happiness looks like the beautiful, colourful fireworks.
Happiness smells like fresh air running in my lungs.
Happiness tastes like sweet, melting chocolate.

Nathan Roberts (6)
Boskenwyn Community Primary School, Helston

A Papaya

A papaya feels like a slippery cow's udder.
A papaya tastes like a juicy strawberry.
A papaya smells yucky like a poo.
A papaya sounds crunchy like biscuits.
A papaya feels slippery like water.

Carson Scott Jeffrey (6)
Brynteg County Primary School, Wrexham

Papaya

A papaya sounds as crunchy as crisps.
A papaya feels as slippy as hugs.
A papaya smells like polish.
A papaya tastes like a chocolate bar.
A papaya looks yellow like the sun.

CJ Richardson (6)
Brynteg County Primary School, Wrexham

What senses did you enjoy reading about on these pages? Colour the symbols.

A Papaya

A papaya tastes like a beautiful flower.
A papaya smells like a yucky fruit.
A papaya looks as green as grass.
A papaya feels slippy like ice.
A papaya sounds as crunchy as paper.

Estera Brudel (6)
Brynteg County Primary School, Wrexham

A Grape

A grape looks like a pear.
A grape tastes like an orange.
A grape feels like a teddy.
A grape smells like a sweet strawberry.
A grape sounds like crunchy crisps.

Lily May Borgerson (6)
Brynteg County Primary School, Wrexham

Papaya

A papaya sounds like crunchy cornflakes.
A papaya tastes like melon on a beach.
A papaya smells like sweet sugar.
A papaya feels like an apple on a stick.
A papaya looks like a pear in a ball.

Lee Williams (6)
Brynteg County Primary School, Wrexham

What senses did you enjoy reading about on these pages? Colour the symbols.

A Papaya

A papaya tastes like fruity apples.
A papaya sounds crunchy like carrots.
A papaya smells like flowers.
A papaya looks juicy like an orange.
A papaya feels soft like skin.

Ioan Prile (6)
Brynteg County Primary School, Wrexham

Senses On Fire

I heard whispering like a spy.
I heard crackling like Rice Krispies.
I felt boiling hot flames.
I felt the flames hot as the sun.
I smelt ash, black as a laptop.
I smelt smoke, white as a piece of paper.
I saw smoke and newspaper.
I saw sticks.
I tasted ash.
I tasted smoke.

Solomon Compton (6)
Crossways Infant School, Bristol

What senses did you enjoy reading about on these pages? Colour the symbols.

Senses Of Fire

I heard Mr Thomas' noise.
I heard popping like popping corn.
I heard the smoke whispering stories to me.
I tasted nothing.
Then I tasted hot, smoky air.
I smelt nothing in the air.
Then I smelt warm, burning fire.
I smelt lots and lots of gas.
I felt my cold, wet bottom.
I felt hot hands.
I felt fiery breath.

Evie Smithson (6)
Crossways Infant School, Bristol

Untitled

Fire sounds like someone whispering to me.
Fire feels like heat burning my hand.
Fire tastes like burning logs and burning paper in your mouth.
You can smell smoky, orange fire.
You see red, yellow and orange, wavy fire.

Harvey Balding (7)
Crossways Infant School, Bristol

What senses did you enjoy reading about on these pages? Colour the symbols.

Fun, Fire And Fun Poetry

I heard snapping like an angry crocodile.
I heard whispering voices like spies telling me a story.
I heard banging like dangerous thunder overhead.
I smelt burnt bacon.
I smelt burnt, hot gas.
I smelt burnt crisps.
I tasted sizzling, hot smoke.
I tasted hot air.
I tasted hot, flaming paper.

Megan Wareing (6)
Crossways Infant School, Bristol

Senses Of A Big Fire

I heard crackling, roaring flames.
I heard whispering, like spies telling me a story.
I tasted smoke like ash.
I tasted fiery air.
I felt smoky air.
I felt fiery breath.
I smelt smoky air.
I smelt lots of gas.
I saw red, yellow and orange flames.
I saw swirling smoke.

Eleanor Grace Wickett (7)
Crossways Infant School, Bristol

What senses did you enjoy reading about on these pages? Colour the symbols.

Senses Of Fire

I heard whispering that was telling me a story.
I heard roaring like a dragon.
I heard roaring like a dinosaur.
I smelt burnt bacon.
I smelt gas and smoke in the air.
I smelt steaming fire burst into the air.

Amilee Monks (6)
Crossways Infant School, Bristol

Eyes, Nose, Hands, Lips, Ears...Fire!

I heard cackling like a witch.
I heard roaring like a tiger.
I heard whispering like a spy.
I felt burning like a bonfire.
I touched hotness like lava.
I saw jumbling flames up in the air.
I saw red, yellow and orange in the air.
I smelt burning air.
I tasted dryness.

Sofiya Perrigo (6)
Crossways Infant School, Bristol

What senses did you enjoy reading about on these pages? Colour the symbols.

Senses Of Fire

Fire smells like a roast dinner.
Fire tastes like burnt toast.
Fire sounds like men snoring.
Fire feels like blankets around me.
Fire looks like leaves swaying.

Lucas Jones (6)
Crossways Infant School, Bristol

Flame Burns Bright

Flames burning bright like smoke blowing in the leaves.
The orange fire wiggles like a worm.
The fire tastes like warm hot chocolate on a winter's day and night.
The fire cracks like popping candy.
The fire looks like leaves blowing in the breeze.

Sophie Swanston (6)
Crossways Infant School, Bristol

Fire

Fire sounds like a meteor shower.
Fire is as warm as some sausages from a barbecue.
Fire looks as big as my birthday cake.
Fire smells like a burning bundle of cloves.
Fire tastes like some overcooked marshmallows and burnt chicken.

Holly Watson (6)
Crossways Infant School, Bristol

What senses did you enjoy reading about on these pages? Colour the symbols.

Fire Senses

Fire sounds like crackling twigs,
Hissing up because they're silly things.
Fire feels like the warm sun,
Heating the Earth until it was done.
Fire looks like orange leaves,
Dancing and prancing as bright as the day.
Fire smells like burning food,
Steaming hot and the twigs are blue.
Fire tastes like hot chocolate,
Warm as lava that isn't stopping.

Sophie Clifton (7)
Crossways Infant School, Bristol

Sycamore Peace Poem

Peace feels like a furry cat
Peace looks like a tiny fairy
Peace sounds like birds singing
Peace tastes like candy hearts
Peace smells like freshly washed clothes.

Sycamore Class (5)
Falconer's Hill Infant School, Daventry

Chestnut Peace Poem

Peace sounds like quiet.
Peace looks like sparkles.
Peace feels like kind hands and snow.
Peace smells like chocolate.
Peace tastes like strawberries.

Chestnut Class (5)
Falconer's Hill Infant School, Daventry

What senses did you enjoy reading about on these pages? Colour the symbols.

Peace

If peace was a colour it would be all the colours of the rainbow
shining beautifully.
If peace was a sound it would be the sound of the birds tweeting and
rushing off
into the white, fluffy clouds.
If peace was an animal it would be a black and white panda bear
swinging off the trees.
If peace was an object it would be a soft and cuddly teddy bear
sitting on my comfy bed.
If peace was a special place it would be the beautiful country park
where I have loads of awesome fun!

Maple Class
Falconer's Hill Infant School, Daventry

Peace

If peace was a sound it would be the laughter of smiling children.
If peace was a material it would be a warm, soft blanket.
If peace was an animal it would be a beautifully patterned butterfly.
If peace was a colour it would be the white of fluffy clouds.
If peace was a special place it would be at home where I feel loved.

Ash Class
Falconer's Hill Infant School, Daventry

What senses did you enjoy reading about on these pages? Colour the symbols.

Peace

Peace is yellow like the sun shining in the bright, blue sky.
Peace is blue, like our world, spinning in space.
Peace is a kite, swaying in the breeze.
Peace is a blanket, soft and cuddly.
Peace is a dolphin, swimming in the calm, blue sea.
Peace is a butterfly, fluttering around my garden.
Peace is honey, sweet as candy.
Peace is hot chocolate, keeping me warm and safe.

Willow Class (7)
Falconer's Hill Infant School, Daventry

War And Peace

War is extreme. Peace is friendship.
War is frightening. Peace is quietness.
War is rough. Peace is kindness.
War is black. Peace is calm.
War is shocking. Peace is sharing.
War is dangerous. Peace is relaxing.
War is loss. Peace is helping.
War is death. Peace is forgiving.

War is heartbreaking. Peace is love.

Oak Class (7)
Falconer's Hill Infant School, Daventry

What senses did you enjoy reading about on these pages? Colour the symbols.

The Moss Woodlands

The moss smells like pine waking me up.
The moss looks like berries hanging in the trees.
The moss sounds like birds tweeting in the trees.
The moss feels like leaves rattling on the ground.
The moss tastes like strawberry sundae in my hand.

Aimee Thomson (7)
Fishermoss School, Aberdeen

The Moss Woodlands

The moss smells like fireworks
The moss looks like birds tweeting in the trees
The moss sounds like the broom rattling in the trees
The moss feels like soft grass
The moss tastes like icicles

Eryn Forbes (7)
Fishermoss School, Aberdeen

The Moss Woodlands

The moss smells like pine, it reminds me of the cold nipping my nose
The moss tastes like icicles making my mouth freezing, so nice and cold
The moss sounds like birds tweeting in the sky
The moss feels like wheat, which reminds me of cereal tickling my fingers
The moss looks like beautiful berries hanging from the trees.

Owen Willox (7)
Fishermoss School, Aberdeen

What senses did you enjoy reading about on these pages? Colour the symbols.

The Moss Woodlands

The moss smells like fresh pine catching my nose
The moss sounds like rattling broom in the wind
The moss feels like soft, smooth trees
The moss looks like spiky thistles
The moss tastes like hot dogs and sandwiches.

Fynn Matthew (7)
Fishermoss School, Aberdeen

The Moss Woodlands

The moss smells like pine cones making me cry,
The moss looks like brown trees,
The moss sounds like birds tweeting,
The moss tastes like chocolate,
The moss feels like thorns hurting my fingers.

Daniel Wilkins (7)
Fishermoss School, Aberdeen

The Moss Woodlands

The moss smells like damp leaves
The moss looks like trees blowing in the wind
The moss sounds like birds tweeting
The moss tastes like wild berries
The moss feels like soft leaves and prickly nettles.

Corey Stephen (7)
Fishermoss School, Aberdeen

What senses did you enjoy reading about on these pages? Colour the symbols.

The Moss Woodlands

The moss smells like pine cones and plants
The moss looks like a garden, the red berries hanging in bunches
The moss tastes like lemonade
The moss sounds like birds whistling in the trees.

Emma Jane Marshall (7)
Fishermoss School, Aberdeen

The Moss Woodland

The moss smells like mud
The moss looks like sparkling leaves
The moss sounds like wind blowing the leaves
The moss feels like soft grass
The moss tastes like cold lemonade.

Al Rizopoulos (7)
Fishermoss School, Aberdeen

The Moss Woodlands

The moss smells like sharp pine
The moss looks like trees shaking
The moss sounds like a broom rattling
The moss feels like thorns prickling my finger
The moss tastes like fizzy lemonade, sparkling in the sun.

Euan Mitchell (7)
Fishermoss School, Aberdeen

What senses did you enjoy reading about on these pages? Colour the symbols.

The Moss Woodland

The moss smells like fresh tree bark tingling past my nose
The moss looks like huge bushes are surrounding me
The moss sounds like tweeting birds singing in the trees
The moss feels like soft petals touching my fingers
The moss tastes like lovely chocolate ice cream touching my lips.

Arran Cameron (7)
Fishermoss School, Aberdeen

The Moss Woodlands

The moss smells like pine
The moss looks like leaves
The moss sounds like birds in the trees
The moss tastes like lemon ice.

Aaron Burns (6)
Fishermoss School, Aberdeen

The Moss Woodlands

The moss smells like damp leaves
The moss looks like beautiful, sparkling grass in the sun
The moss sounds like a rattling broom in the wind
The moss feels like lovely, soft wheat
The moss tastes like cold ice cream, so sweet.

Eilidh Mitchell (7)
Fishermoss School, Aberdeen

What senses did you enjoy reading about on these pages? Colour the symbols.

The Moss Woodlands

The moss looks like birds singing sweetly
The moss tastes like lovely, tasty sweets
The moss sounds like pine cones falling down
The moss feels like flowers twinkling like stars
The moss smells like plants swishing in the wind.

.Isabella Duncan (7)
Fishermoss School, Aberdeen

The Moss Woodland

The moss smells like damp leaves
The moss sounds like rattling broom
The moss looks like birds singing in the trees
The moss tastes like chocolate brownies
The moss feels like spiky thistles.

Ahmet Keshiyev (7)
Fishermoss School, Aberdeen

The Moss Woodlands

The moss smells like fresh nature
The moss looks like lovely red raspberries growing
The moss feels like smooth, sweet grass and prickly nettles
The moss sounds like crackling leaves
The moss tastes like watery lettuce.

Aaliyah Smith (7)
Fishermoss School, Aberdeen

What senses did you enjoy reading about on these pages? Colour the symbols.

30

The Moss Woodlands

The moss smells like pine and makes me happy
The moss looks like red, shining berries
The moss sounds like rattling broom pods
The moss feels like squelchy mud
The moss tastes like sparkling lemonade.

Amy Walker (6)
Fishermoss School, Aberdeen

The Moss Woodlands

The moss smells like leaves, smells like the wood
The moss looks like snail trails sparkling in the sun
The moss feels like nettles stinging
The moss tastes like orange ice cream
The moss sounds through my ear.

Jay Thompson (7)
Fishermoss School, Aberdeen

Untitled

Autumn sounds like the wind blowing with a strong blow.
Autumn feels like eating lots of toffee pudding.
Autumn looks like a cold country.
Autumn smells like tractors spreading dung.
Autumn tastes like eating candy at Halloween.

Callum McInnes (7)
Glenbervie School, Stonehaven

What senses did you enjoy reading about on these pages? Colour the symbols.

Autumn Cottage

Autumn smells like hot fire
Autumn feels like the chilly wind
Autumn looks like leaves falling down
Autumn tastes like sweet, sticky jam.

Connor Jarvie (7)
Glenbervie School, Stonehaven

Autumn Poem

Leaves go crunching when you step on them in the autumn.
You can see the leaves falling off the trees.
In autumn the leaves change colour.
In autumn you can eat apple pie.

Amy McPherson (6)
Glenbervie School, Stonehaven

Autumn Poem

Fireworks bang and wind whistles
Autumn feels like sticky toffee and warm fires
Autumn looks like pink skies at night
Autumn smells like strong manure and hot fires
Autumn tastes like sweet, sticky jam.

Jake Owen (7)
Glenbervie School, Stonehaven

What senses did you enjoy reading about on these pages? Colour the symbols.

Autumn Poem

Autumn sounds like fireworks banging in the sky.
Autumn feels like muddy tatties and the cold air.
Autumn looks like leaves falling from the trees.
Autumn smells like sticky toffee apples.
Autumn tastes like candy at Halloween.

Hannah Miller (7)
Glenbervie School, Stonehaven

Autumn Poem

Autumn sounds like leaves crunching under your feet and fireworks banging.
Autumn feels like spiky conkers and a big spade digging.
Autumn looks like leaves changing colours and geese quacking.
Autumn smells like soil turned over and sweet candy at Halloween.
Autumn tastes like apple pie and sticky toffee apples.

Stuart Jamieson (7)
Glenbervie School, Stonehaven

Untitled

I could hear the engines going *pffff* and *bang!*
I could feel the smooth, circular steering wheel.
I could taste fear in my mouth.
I could see myself blasting off into space very quickly.
I was going 17,000 miles per hour!

Danny Hall (6)
Hambleton CE Primary School, Selby

What senses did you enjoy reading about on these pages? Colour the symbols.

Cartwheel In Space

I can see nothing but the Earth.
I can see Florida and India and Africa and Jamaica.
I saw Jupiter and Saturn, Mars and Venus,
Mercury and Uranus.
I can see smoke.
Often I don't see the moon.
I can see the bright stars in the sky,
As bright as the sun.
I saw Jupiter and Saturn cartwheel in space.

Izzy Summerton (6)
Hambleton CE Primary School, Selby

What You Do

I can see clouds that look like twirling waves.
I can smell smoke burning.
I can taste lots of flames.
I can feel hope.

Seth Harvey (6)
Hambleton CE Primary School, Selby

What senses did you enjoy reading about on these pages? Colour the symbols.

Space Trip

I quickly blast up to space!
I can taste the cheesy moon.
I can smell the strong smoke.
I can see the colourful Earth.
In the sky the clouds are as white as snow.
I can hear a flying saucer.
I can smell fear.
I can hear the engines roaring.
I can feel the flashing buttons on the space shuttle.
Living in space is fun.

Jessica Glover (6)
Hambleton CE Primary School, Selby

Rocket Ship

I can see the gigantic Earth spinning all around me
And it is making me dizzy a lot.
I can feel the ginormous gigantic rocket blasting off to space.
I can hear the roaring rocket lifting up into space
That goes on and on forever and ever.
I can hear the roaring, shiny rocket getting ready to blast off
To the fluffy, white, clear clouds.
I can taste a lot of fear.
I can smell big, grey dust that is tickling my nose like a feather.

Sophie Bright (6)
Hambleton CE Primary School, Selby

What senses did you enjoy reading about on these pages? Colour the symbols.

Rocket Boost

I can hear '5, 4, 3, 2, 1, blast off!'
I can feel the soft space sky.
I can see the wavy, white sea that looks like clouds.
I can smell the fiery smoke.
I can taste the moon rock.
I can taste the water from my eye.

Tia Hardy (6)
Hambleton CE Primary School, Selby

The Blast Off Poem

I can taste the pancakes like bread.
I can smell the huge moon.
I can touch the rough moon rock.
I can see the huge world around me.
I can hear the rumbling boosters shooting up.

Freya Ruddock (6)
Hambleton CE Primary School, Selby

The Planet

I can see hot, flaming fire coming out of the red rocket.
I can hear the countdown from 10.
You could probably taste the moon.
I can taste fear.
You could probably taste moon rocks.
My mouth touched the moon and it was hard.
I can smell fear coming out of the bottom.
I can see flaming hot fire coming out of the bottom.
I can smell fire.
The flaming, hot fire is coming out of the exploding moon.

Erin McMichan (6)
Hambleton CE Primary School, Selby

What senses did you enjoy reading about on these pages? Colour the symbols.

A Poem Using Our Senses

Anger is angry
It tastes like cheese
It smells like stinky socks
Anger looks like angry people
It sounds like fire
Anger is a madman.

Caleb Quinn (6)
Holy Family Primary School, Londonderry

Write A Poem Using Our Senses

Anger is a black volcano.
It tastes like stew mixed with melted cheese.
Anger smells like vomit.
Anger looks like a dark black sky.
Anger sounds like a big drum.
Anger is angry.

Jake Henry (6)
Holy Family Primary School, Londonderry

Sadness

Sadness is a very sad thing to have.
It tastes like a raindrop that falls into a bird's mouth.
Sadness is the smell of off milk.
Sadness looks like a flower that has died.
It sounds like a very, very sad thing.
Sadness is a deer that has just been shot.

Riain Barr (6)
Holy Family Primary School, Londonderry

What senses did you enjoy reading about on these pages? Colour the symbols.

Sadness

Sadness is a time when you're feeling sad.
It tastes like a squashy blueberry.
Sadness is the smell of a rubbish bin.
Sadness looks like people wet and crying.
It sounds like a place where there are no people.
Sadness is a cold, sad day.

Lucie-Rose Crossan (7)
Holy Family Primary School, Londonderry

The Lonely World

The world smells like cows eating grapes.
The world looks like light for space.
The world sounds like gentle humming.
The world feels ice cold.
The world tastes like cheese and biscuits.

Dawid Lutynski (6)
Holy Trinity CE Primary & Nursery School, Richmond

The Lunch Hall

The lunch hall smells like delicious food
The lunch hall looks full of people eating
The lunch hall feels like hard floors under my feet
The lunch hall sounds like ten elephants stomping.

Emma Lidblom (6)
Holy Trinity CE Primary & Nursery School, Richmond

What senses did you enjoy reading about on these pages? Colour the symbols.

Eyes, Mouths, Hands, Noses And Ears In The Playground

The playground smells like stones and forests
The playground tastes like sweets
The playground sounds like children shouting
The playground feels like dress-up picnics
The playground looks like happy children.

Costya Simonov (6)
Holy Trinity CE Primary & Nursery School, Richmond

Colourful Playground

The playground smells like wind blowing through the parks.
The playground looks like huge climbing frames.
The playground feels like bumping hills going up and down
The playground sounds noisy like children shouting
The playground tastes like birthday cake.

Madeleine Skager (6)
Holy Trinity CE Primary & Nursery School, Richmond

Rugby World Cup

I can hear the noise of the crowds
I imagine touching the golden trophy
I can see players snatching the ball
I can smell the blood on the field
I can taste the excitement of the game
I love rugby.

Willem De Haan (6)
Holy Trinity CE Primary & Nursery School, Richmond

What senses did you enjoy reading about on these pages? Colour the symbols.

The Yummy Lunch Hall

The lunch hall smells like yummy noodles
The lunch hall looks like busy chefs cooking
The lunch hall sounds like lots of voices
The lunch hall feels like metal knives
The lunch hall tastes like fish.

Kamran Shaha (6)
Holy Trinity CE Primary & Nursery School, Richmond

London, The Best

I can taste the excitement on the street
I can hear Big Ben going *ding dong!*
I can feel the crowd
I can see the tall buildings on the skyline
I can smell the gassy cars
This is my London.

Sam Badawi (6)
Holy Trinity CE Primary & Nursery School, Richmond

Noisy Playground

The playground smells like the trees
The playground looks like bushes swaying
The playground sounds like children playing
The playground feels like a climbing frame
The playground tastes like the air.

Tanvi Mishra (6)
Holy Trinity CE Primary & Nursery School, Richmond

What senses did you enjoy reading about on these pages? Colour the symbols.

Autumn Time

Autumn smells like wet leaves
Autumn looks very cold
Autumn feels like wet bark
Autumn sounds quiet like at night
Autumn tastes like delicious hot chocolate.

Harriet Askham (6)
Holy Trinity CE Primary & Nursery School, Richmond

The Sparkling Love

Friendliness smells like toffee and sweets
Friendliness looks like lots of hugs
Friendliness sounds like lots of kind words
Friendliness feels like a warm hug
Friendliness tastes like sweet candy.

Olivia Moher (6)
Holy Trinity CE Primary & Nursery School, Richmond

Huge London

London smells like stinky fish
London looks like the huge Shard
London sounds like busy people shouting like thunder
London feels like my yummy food
London tastes like see-through air.

Caleb Connor (6)
Holy Trinity CE Primary & Nursery School, Richmond

What senses did you enjoy reading about on these pages? Colour the symbols.

Empty Plate

The lunch hall smells like sausages cooking,
The lunch hall tastes like the crust of fish fingers,
The lunch hall sounds like chips crunching in mouths,
The lunch hall tables feel as smooth as a banana,
The lunch hall looks like people getting and eating their food,
But my plate is empty. Ha ha.

Matin MacDermott (7)
Holy Trinity CE Primary & Nursery School, Richmond

London

London smells as clean as a tidy bedroom,
London sounds busy as a crowd,
London feels hard and rough,
London looks big,
London tastes of sour cabbages!

Zoe Lennon (7)
Holy Trinity CE Primary & Nursery School, Richmond

Pear And William

Pears smell delicious,
Pears smell like fresh fruit
Pears feel like hard stone
Pears look like green leaves
Pears sound like crunching on an autumn day.

William Cohn (7)
Holy Trinity CE Primary & Nursery School, Richmond

What senses did you enjoy reading about on these pages? Colour the symbols.

Friendliness

Friendliness smells like hearts
Friendliness tastes like hot chocolate
Friendliness sounds like children talking
Friendliness feels like children
Friendliness looks like children running.

Kennosuke Ken Maeda (7)
Holy Trinity CE Primary & Nursery School, Richmond

Richmond Park

It smells like grass growing tall.
It tastes like frost on the ground.
It sounds like the birds flying all around me.
It feels like the bark on the trees.
It looks like leaves falling off the trees.

Sonny Matthews (6)
Holy Trinity CE Primary & Nursery School, Richmond

Our Friendliness

Friendliness feels like happiness never leaving you.
Friendliness sounds like the help coming your way.
Friendliness smells like fresh, cool air, helping you breathe,
Friendliness looks like your nice friends, rushing to play,
Friendliness tastes like cake, it's your favourite!

Lili Eszenyi (6)
Holy Trinity CE Primary & Nursery School, Richmond

What senses did you enjoy reading about on these pages? Colour the symbols.

Friendliness

Friendliness tastes like sweet birthday cake,
Friendliness sounds like laughter,
Friendliness looks like a big smile,
Friendliness smells beautiful,
Friendliness feels happy and kind.

Caden Behr (6)
Holy Trinity CE Primary & Nursery School, Richmond

The Pear

The pear looks as green as a pear shaped balloon
The pear tastes juicy
The pear sounds as quiet as a mouse
The pear feels a bit rough
The pear smells sweet!

Elliot Jardine (6)
Holy Trinity CE Primary & Nursery School, Richmond

London

London smells like food,
London tastes sweet like fruit,
London sounds like cars and buses,
London feels rough and hard,
London looks busy!

Beth Anderson (6)
Holy Trinity CE Primary & Nursery School, Richmond

What senses did you enjoy reading about on these pages? Colour the symbols.

The Pear

The pear is quiet as a gust of wind,
The pear is as juicy as an orange,
The pear is as rough as tarmac,
The pear is as round as feet,
The pear is as sweet as a piece of candy!

Oscar Allbut (7)
Holy Trinity CE Primary & Nursery School, Richmond

Bustling London

London sounds like bustling cars driving through the streets
London feels hard like bricks in a house.
London looks like a big, beautiful city.
London tastes like sausages on fire.
London smells like flowers in a garden.

Maximilian Lennox Klos Dias (6)
Holy Trinity CE Primary & Nursery School, Richmond

Busy London

London sounds like busy cars and planes flying overhead,
Big trains rumbling over bridges and boats on the River Thames,
London smells like car fumes, people and sweets.
London looks like tall buildings, stations, bridges, cars and buses,
London feels like train buttons, shop windows and bread.
London tastes like sweets, juicy and sandwiches.

Alexander Pooley (6)
Holy Trinity CE Primary & Nursery School, Richmond

What senses did you enjoy reading about on these pages? Colour the symbols.

The Busy Playground

The playground smells like sausages and mash,
The playground looks like a colourful adventure,
The playground sounds like a baby crying and screaming,
The playground feels like monkey bars,
The playground tastes like sausages and chips.

Layla Geisler (6)
Holy Trinity CE Primary & Nursery School, Richmond

Best London

London smells like wealthy people buying expensive clothes,
London looks like a big chocolate sweet,
London sounds like racing cars patrolling the city,
London feels like extremely sticky tape,
London tastes like yummy pizza.

Jonah Neal (6)
Holy Trinity CE Primary & Nursery School, Richmond

Untitled

I am jelly.
Wibble wobble jelly on a plate.
Strawberry jelly?
Jodie is eating some jelly.
Jelly is so good because it gives you muscles and a moustache.

Vincent Window-Beardon (5)
Horizon Primary Academy, Swanley

What senses did you enjoy reading about on these pages? Colour the symbols.

Jelly

Jelly has a good taste.
My dad is a good cook.
It is wobbly.
I lick the jelly.
It taste like strawberry jelly.

Liam Chick (5)
Horizon Primary Academy, Swanley

Jelly

Jelly in my belly.
Jelly in my belly.
It is red, tastes like strawberry.

Harvey Michael Evans (5)
Horizon Primary Academy, Swanley

Untitled

Jelly is wobbly and it can be green or orange.
It smells like strawberries.
It smells like apples.
It is tasty if you suck it.
It falls off your spoon.
It is drippy and drops.
If it drops on the table it makes a sound like rain,
If it drips on the ground.

Amy Harbour-Chilcott (5)
Horizon Primary Academy, Swanley

What senses did you enjoy reading about on these pages? Colour the symbols.

Super Senses

It looks like chocolate.
It tastes like bananas.
It feels squishy.
It smells like banana.
It sounds crunchy.

Henry Tapson (5)
Horizon Primary Academy, Swanley

Untitled

Jelly is strawberry.
Jelly is quiet.
Jelly is soft, yummy, yummy!
I thinks it tastes likes strawberry.
it smells like sweets.

Roxanne Parker (5)
Horizon Primary Academy, Swanley

Untitled

It tastes like water.
It looks like rain.
I think it is made in clouds from more rain.
It smells wet.
It feels wet.

Ayomide Osibona (5)
Horizon Primary Academy, Swanley

What senses did you enjoy reading about on these pages? Colour the symbols.

Untitled

Rain is so cold
When it looks like a blue sky it is not.
When you feel rain it does not feel like slime,
But jelly is.
It is yummy, yummy and scrummy too.

Lexi Kennard (5)
Horizon Primary Academy, Swanley

Autumn Time

I can see the colourful leaves floating to the ground.
I can touch squishy marshmallows.
I can smell cracking bonfires.
I can hear crunching leaves under my feet.
I can taste burning hot dogs.

Ryan Todd (5)
Iron Acton CE Primary School, Bristol

Harvest

I can taste juicy blackberries.
I can see the leaves drifting off the trees.
I can feel the round apples.
I can smell smoke.
I can hear crackling bonfires smoking.

Rosie Webber (5)
Iron Acton CE Primary School, Bristol

What senses did you enjoy reading about on these pages? Colour the symbols.

Autumn Senses

I can hear the crackling fireworks.
I can feel the round apples.
I can see the squirrels collecting acorns for the autumn.
I can smell a smoky bonfire.
I can taste the sweet, juicy berries growing all around us.

Owen McPartland (5)
Iron Acton CE Primary School, Bristol

I Love Autumn

I can see the leaves falling.
I can taste hot dogs.
I can feel the air on my face.
I can hear the birds.
I can smell the bonfire.

Theo Foote (5)
Iron Acton CE Primary School, Bristol

Autumn Fun

I can feel the crunching leaves.
I can eat the hot hot dog.
I can hear the crunching leaves in the breeze.
I can smell the crackling bonfire.
I can see the cheeky squirrels having fun.

Ruben Hunt (6)
Iron Acton CE Primary School, Bristol

What senses did you enjoy reading about on these pages? Colour the symbols.

Autumn

I can hear the whistling birds.
I can smell bonfires.
I can taste blackberries.
I can see cheeky squirrels hiding acorns.
I can touch squishy marshmallows.

Katrina Roberts (5)
Iron Acton CE Primary School, Bristol

Autumn

A corns falling off the tall trees.
U p the tree bugs you will see
T ree branches blowing in the wind
U p in the sky sunset will shine
M oss growing up all of the trees
N o leaves to be seen.

Lucinda McLeod
Lainshaw Primary School, Kilmarnock

Autumn

A ll the leaves falling
U p in the sky the sun shines
T rees changing colour
U nderneath the frost were leaves
M y body gets cold
N ow the frost starts to cover the leaves.

Capree Jovanna Powell (8)
Lainshaw Primary School, Kilmarnock

What senses did you enjoy reading about on these pages? Colour the symbols.

Autumn

A utumn trees, falling leaves.
U nder the ground there are animals.
T rees are falling on the ground.
U p the trees there are birds.
M y garden is covered in leaves.
N ot much sun comes out at autumn.

Marni McPherson (8)
Lainshaw Primary School, Kilmarnock

Autumn

A utumn, happy children playing in the dead leaves.
U nhappy when autumn goes away.
T all trees up in the sky.
U p in the tree bugs you will see.
M idnight in the morning.
N ight grows dark and wolves howl loud.

MacKenzie King
Lainshaw Primary School, Kilmarnock

Autumn

A ll the rattling leaves
U p the trees bugs you will see
T he branches swaying in the breeze
U p in the sky sunset you see
M oss growing all around
N ight sky falls early.

Jessica Dougall
Lainshaw Primary School, Kilmarnock

What senses did you enjoy reading about on these pages? Colour the symbols.

Autumn

A corns falling on my head.
U p in the trees the leaves waving.
T rees reflecting off the water.
U nder the ground the roots of the trees are growing.
M e and my friends playing in the leaves.
N ettles swirling next to the tree, I and my friends are avoiding.

Paul Wilkie
Lainshaw Primary School, Kilmarnock

Autumn

A corns falling off tall trees.
U pside down, hanging on, then jumping off.
T he birds tweeting in the beautiful trees.
U nderneath the crunchy leaves while playing.
M oon shining in the evening sky.
N ettles in the deep, dark forest at night.

Zoe Templeton
Lainshaw Primary School, Kilmarnock

Autumn

A utumn leaves falling from the trees
U p the tree you will see birds
T ea warming up in the breeze
U nderneath the bugs are having a feast
M ums and dads tucking boys and girls in bed
N ight falling quick.

Rohan Harkins
Lainshaw Primary School, Kilmarnock

What senses did you enjoy reading about on these pages? Colour the symbols.

Autumn

A ll the acorns on the ground
U p the tree leaves are falling
T he leaves swaying side to side
U nder the tree branches is a nest with baby birds
M agical leaves are changing colours
N ight comes and the leaves fly in the strong wind.

Millie Gebbie
Lainshaw Primary School, Kilmarnock

Autumn

A ll the grass gets frozen
U p in the trees birds are singing loudly
T he sun shining on the trees
U nder the ground animals are sleeping
M y garden is all frozen
N o path to be seen.

Alexa MacTaggart
Lainshaw Primary School, Kilmarnock

Autumn

A ll the dark nights are here
U p in the tree is a big mystery
T ime for harvest!
U nder the leaves is so fun!
M y family all cuddling on the couch
N ight falls fast.

Heather Mary McAllister (8)
Lainshaw Primary School, Kilmarnock

What senses did you enjoy reading about on these pages? Colour the symbols.

Autumn

A ll the beautiful leaves falling.
U p in the sky the birds fly high.
T rees reflecting off the water.
U nder the grass the dirt is wet.
M illions of leaves falling off the trees.
N ot as many animals out this month.

Brodie Wilson
Lainshaw Primary School, Kilmarnock

Autumn

A utumn trees and falling leaves
U p above the birds soar beautifully
T winkling stars come out much faster
U nexpected rains come pouring down
M ysterious colours on lots of leaves
N ot much sun comes out at autumn.

Peter Niven (7)
Lainshaw Primary School, Kilmarnock

Autumn

A baby fox plays in a forest
U p in the tree lives a baby bird
T umbling down the hill are hedgehogs
U nderneath the deep, dark hole it is so damp
M agic in the trees
N utshells left by squirrels.

Keira McNelis (8)
Lainshaw Primary School, Kilmarnock

What senses did you enjoy reading about on these pages? Colour the symbols.

Autumn

A utumn, the brown leaves
U p the trees bugs you will see
T ree branches moving in the breeze
U p above birds are flying
M oths are flying all around
N ight falls, hear the wolves howling.

Allan Brodie
Lainshaw Primary School, Kilmarnock

Autumn

A corns falling off the trees
U p above birds are flying
T ree branches moving in the wind
U p in the tree moss you will see
M others putting children to bed
N ight falls and the wolves howl.

Cassie Rooney
Lainshaw Primary School, Kilmarnock

Bonfire Night

I can see fire.
I can taste cupcakes.
I can touch sparklers.
I can smell smoke.
I can hear fireworks.

Leo Norbury (5)
Pontefract Orchard Head Junior And Infant School, Pontefract

What senses did you enjoy reading about on these pages? Colour the symbols.

Bonfire Night

I can see fireworks.
I can taste hot chocolate.
I can hear crackers.
I can smell hot dogs.
I can touch sparklers.

Sienna Sinclair (5)
Pontefract Orchard Head Junior And Infant School, Pontefract

Bonfire Night

I can touch sparklers.
I can hear banging.
I can see fireworks.
I can smell smoke.
I can taste marshmallows.

Tyler Stephen Dillon Montgomery (5)
Pontefract Orchard Head Junior And Infant School, Pontefract

Bonfire Night

I can see fireworks.
I can taste burgers.
I can touch sparklers.
I can smell smoke.
I can hear whistling.

Joshua Pearce (5)
Pontefract Orchard Head Junior And Infant School, Pontefract

What senses did you enjoy reading about on these pages? Colour the symbols.

Bonfire Night

I can smell hot chocolate.
I can touch sparklers.
I can see fireworks.
I can hear banging fireworks.
I can taste hot dogs.

Ethan Smith (5)
Pontefract Orchard Head Junior And Infant School, Pontefract

Bonfire Night

I can taste toffee apples.
I can feel sparklers.
I can see the fireworks.
I can smell smoke.
I can hear the crackling fire.

Millie G (5)
Pontefract Orchard Head Junior And Infant School, Pontefract

Bonfire Night

I can see a big fire and a big firework exploding.
I can hear the fire booming and it sizzling.
I can smell the giant fire.
I can taste the cookies.
I can touch sparklers.

Millen Jay Deravairere (5)
Pontefract Orchard Head Junior And Infant School, Pontefract

What senses did you enjoy reading about on these pages? Colour the symbols.

Bonfire Night

I can see fireworks banging.
I can hear the fire crackling.
I can smell candyfloss.
I can taste hot chocolate.
I can touch sparklers.

Maisie Gregson (5)
Pontefract Orchard Head Junior And Infant School, Pontefract

Bonfire Night

I can see fire exploding in the sky.
I can taste marshmallow sandwiches.
I can touch lovely sparklers.
I can smell hot dogs and chocolate apples.
I can hear the fire crackling.

Edward Raw (5)
Pontefract Orchard Head Junior And Infant School, Pontefract

Bonfire Night

I can see fiery flames.
I can hear fireworks crackling.
I can smell jacket potatoes.
I can taste marshmallows.
I can touch the food.

Olivia Jane Watton (5)
Pontefract Orchard Head Junior And Infant School, Pontefract

What senses did you enjoy reading about on these pages? Colour the symbols.

Bonfire Night

I can taste hot dogs,
I can see the bonfire crackling.
I can feel the smooth sparklers,
I can hear the whistling fireworks.
I can smell the fire's smoke.

Kian Mark Maundrill (5)
Pontefract Orchard Head Junior And Infant School, Pontefract

Bonfire Night

I can see the fireworks in the sky.
I can hear the people talking.
I can smell ice cream.
I can taste chocolate milk.
I can touch the sparklers.

Maria Rodzierwicz (5)
Pontefract Orchard Head Junior And Infant School, Pontefract

Bonfire Night

I can see fireworks.
I can hear the bonfire.
I can smell chocolate apples.
I can taste candyfloss.
I can touch sparklers.

Lisa Krasauskas (5)
Pontefract Orchard Head Junior And Infant School, Pontefract

What senses did you enjoy reading about on these pages? Colour the symbols.

Bonfire Night

We can see fireworks dancing in the sky.
We can hear the fire hissing like a snake.
We can smell toasted marshmallows.
We can taste hot dogs and yummy burgers.
We can touch sparklers as light as the sun.

Callum Cartwright (6)
Pontefract Orchard Head Junior And Infant School, Pontefract

Bonfire Night

On Bonfire night, we can see exploding fireworks.
We can hear fireworks going *kapow, fizz, pop, bang!*
We can smell smoke.
We can taste cupcakes.
We can touch sparklers.

Layla-Jaimes Carson (6)
Pontefract Orchard Head Junior And Infant School, Pontefract

Bonfire Night

On Bonfire night we can see fireworks exploding in the night sky.
We can hear the fire going *bang!*
I can smell pink candyfloss.
I can taste hot chocolate.
I can touch sparklers.

Jasmine Harrison (5)
Pontefract Orchard Head Junior And Infant School, Pontefract

What senses did you enjoy reading about on these pages? Colour the symbols.

Bonfire Night

I can see fireworks.
I can taste hot dogs.
I can touch sparkler.
I can smell burgers.
I can hear fireworks.

Frayah Blackburn (5)
Pontefract Orchard Head Junior And Infant School, Pontefract

Bonfire Night

I can taste hot dogs.
I can touch sparklers.
I can smell smoke.
I can hear fire exploding.
I can see fireworks.

Liam Joseph William Holdsworth (5)
Pontefract Orchard Head Junior And Infant School, Pontefract

Bonfire Night

I can taste hot dogs.
I can hear fireworks banging.
I can touch sparklers.
I can smell smoke.
I can see the bonfire.

Cambell Hunton (6)
Pontefract Orchard Head Junior And Infant School, Pontefract

What senses did you enjoy reading about on these pages? Colour the symbols.

Bonfire Night

I can taste toffee apples. I can see different colours.
I can hear fire crackling.
I can touch sparklers.
I can smell smoke.

M B (5)
Pontefract Orchard Head Junior And Infant School, Pontefract

Bonfire Night

I can hear fireworks.
I can see people.
I can touch sparklers.
I can taste toffee apples.
I can smell smoke.

Harry Shaw (6)
Pontefract Orchard Head Junior And Infant School, Pontefract

Bonfire Night

I can hear fire crackling.
I can touch sparklers.
I can taste chocolate apples.
I can see fireworks.
I can smell hot dogs.

Alfie Widdowson (5)
Pontefract Orchard Head Junior And Infant School, Pontefract

Bonfire Night

I can see fireworks.
I can taste burgers.
I can touch sparklers.
I can hear the fire.
I can smell hot dogs.

William James Croft (5)
Pontefract Orchard Head Junior And Infant School, Pontefract

What senses did you enjoy reading about on these pages? Colour the symbols.

Autumn

Autumn smells like trees with leaves falling
Autumn tastes like freshly cooked mushrooms
Autumn sounds like birds singing
Autumn feels like colourful leaves brushing you as they fall
Autumn looks like grass with water on.

Zara Upton (6)
Palmers Cross Primary School, Wolverhampton

My Five Senses

Autumn smells like hot chocolate
Autumn tastes like baked apple pie
Autumn sounds like the birds flapping their wings
Autumn feels like the wind blowing on my face
Autumn looks like the leaves falling off the trees.

Tianna Esther Sterling (6)
Palmers Cross Primary School, Wolverhampton

Autumn House Warming

Autumn smells like warm soup
Autumn tastes like hot chocolate when it's cold
Autumn sounds like the wind blowing
Autumn feels like stones slipping through your hands
Autumn looks like the leaves falling from the trees.

Serayah Llewellyn-Brown (6)
Palmers Cross Primary School, Wolverhampton

What senses did you enjoy reading about on these pages? Colour the symbols.

Autumn

Autumn smells like marshmallows cooking
Autumn tastes like hot soup on a cold day
Autumn sounds like leaves crunching
Autumn feels hard like a cardboard box
Autumn looks amazing with fireworks at night.

Misbah Chowdhury (7)
Palmers Cross Primary School, Wolverhampton

Autumn Poem

Autumn smells like marshmallows roasting
Autumn tastes like hot chocolate on a cold evening
Autumn sounds like the birds tweeting as they fly away
Autumn feels like wind in my hair
Autumn looks like leaves falling down.

Mia Alex Sandhu (6)
Palmers Cross Primary School, Wolverhampton

Autumn

In autumn it smells like muddy shoes all over the house
In autumn it tastes like hot chocolate all day long
In autumn it sounds like the trees moving in the wind
In autumn it feels like rain falling on your face
In autumn you can see leaves all over the floor.

Kairo Williams (6)
Palmers Cross Primary School, Wolverhampton

What senses did you enjoy reading about on these pages? Colour the symbols.

Autumn

Autumn smells like burning fire
Autumn tastes like hot chocolate when it's cold
Autumn sounds like rain banging the windows
Autumn feels like leaves brushing you as they fall
Autumn looks like colourful fireworks in the sky.

Liam Beaumont-Pilgrim (6)
Palmers Cross Primary School, Wolverhampton

Autumn Smell

Autumn smells like hot chocolate
Autumn tastes like hot dinners
Autumn sounds like the noisy wind blowing
Autumn feels like rain spitting on my face
Autumn looks like trees rocking in the wind.

Daniel-Lee Cund (6)
Palmers Cross Primary School, Wolverhampton

Tigers

Tigers sound like a big noise of roaring.
Tigers feel like a very fierce tiger.
Tigers look like soft fur and anger.
Tigers smell like yummy, salty chips.
Tigers taste like a delicious orange.

Ajai Tanve (6)
Redwood Primary School, Derby

What senses did you enjoy reading about on these pages? Colour the symbols.

The Seaside

The seaside sounds like the whooshing waves.
The seaside feels soft.
The seaside looks like I'm looking at the water.
The seaside smells like old dust.
The seaside tastes like salt and is hard.

Tanvi Parigi (6)
Redwood Primary School, Derby

Apples

Apples sound crunchy when you bite them.
Apples feel like little balls.
Apples taste like a crunchy, juicy, sweet fruit that you can eat.
Apples look like red, scrumptious fruit.
Apples feel like fresh, smooth skin.

Dylan Holland (6)
Redwood Primary School, Derby

My Jungle Poem

Animals sound like an elephant trumpeting,
Animals feel like a lion's mane,
Animals look like a giraffe's long neck,
Animals smell like the long, yellow grass,
Animals taste like the meat of a tiger.

Kan Adekunle (6)
Redwood Primary School, Derby

What senses did you enjoy reading about on these pages? Colour the symbols.

Ballet Poem

Ballet sounds like soft music and tapping sounds.
Ballet looks like pink dresses floating.
Ballet tastes like pink ice cream.
Ballet feels like ballet shoes, which feel like a pillow.
Ballet smells like air.

Lily Boyden (6)
Redwood Primary School, Derby

My Superhero Poem

Superheroes sound like whooshing through the sky.
Superheroes feel like yummy candyfloss.
Superheroes look like they need to save the world.
Superheroes smell like pineapple.
Superheroes taste like hard pork.

Chaise Hackney (6)
Redwood Primary School, Derby

The Snowman Poem

The snowman sounds like snowflakes falling down lightly.
The snowman feels like very slushy fun.
The snowman looks like balls piling up.
The snowman smells like a raspberry ice cream.
The snowman tastes like the icy carrot that is freezing my mouth.

Joseph Smith (6)
Redwood Primary School, Derby

What senses did you enjoy reading about on these pages? Colour the symbols.

My Winter Poem

Winter sounds like ice twinkling in a cave.
Winter feels like soft snow.
Winter smells like delicious hot chocolate.
Winter tastes like icicles.

Amayah Javed (6)
Redwood Primary School, Derby

Winter

Winter sounds like snowflakes falling down.
Winter feels very, very cold.
Winter looks like a giant snowball.
Winter smells like an ice lolly.
Winter tastes like ice.

Stefan Chanev (6)
Redwood Primary School, Derby

Apples

Apples sounds like a worm wiggling under my feet.
Apples feels like a worm crunching my apples.
Apples look like a worm eating my lunch.
Apples smell like a worm who was lying.

Urminder Dhillon (6)
Redwood Primary School, Derby

What senses did you enjoy reading about on these pages? Colour the symbols.

My Panda Poetry

A panda sounds like a person crunching an apple.
A panda feels like a soft, gentle pillow.
A panda looks like a black and white zebra.
A panda smells like summer breeze and a sprinkle of winter breeze.
A panda tastes like fair skin and our hair!

Priya Thandi (7)
Redwood Primary School, Derby

Apple Poem

Apples sound like leaves crunching
Apples feel hard and smooth
Apples look like big, hard buttons.
Apples smell juicy.
Apples taste like a scrumptious birthday cake.

Zylah Browne (6)
Redwood Primary School, Derby

My Summer Poem

Summer sounds hot, spicy burning hotpot.
Summer feels like a hot, fiery, spicy ball.
Summer looks like an evil fireball coming to me.
Summer smells like Bonfire Night exploding.
Summer tastes like chocolate ice cream.

Pavandeep Chungh (6)
Redwood Primary School, Derby

What senses did you enjoy reading about on these pages? Colour the symbols.

The Tooth Fairy Poem

The tooth fairy sounds like she is singing a lovely tune.
The tooth fairy feels like she is kissing you on the cheek.
The tooth fairy looks like a shining diamond.
The tooth fairy smells like glitter falling on your nose.
The tooth fairy tastes like sugar.

Tom Adelkunle (6)
Redwood Primary School, Derby

The Appetising Apple

Apples sound like singing in my ear.
Apples feel like tree wood.
Apples look like red and yellow stickers.
Apples smell like sweet sugar candy.
Apples taste like sweet strawberries.

Leila Mae Elliott (6)
Redwood Primary School, Derby

When The Snow Falls

When the snow falls,
I can see a large snowman.
When the snow falls,
I can touch fluffy snowballs.
When the snow falls,
I can smell a smoky fire.
When the snow falls,
I can taste warm sausages.
When the snow falls,
I can hear owls hooting.

Mason Bowles (5)
St James' CE Primary School, St. Helens

What senses did you enjoy reading about on these pages? Colour the symbols.

71

When The Snow Falls

When the snow falls,
I can see snowballs.
I can touch a snowball.
I can smell a fire.
I can taste soup.
I can hear laughter.

Ben Conway-Henthorn (5)
St James' CE Primary School, St. Helens

Untitled

Standing in a snowy field
I can see white trees.
Standing in a snowy field
I can touch spiky grass.
Standing in a snowy field
I can smell hot chocolate.
Standing in a snowy field
I can taste warm tea.
Standing in a snowy field
I can hear trees blowing.

Olivia-Mai Davies (5)
St James' CE Primary School, St. Helens

What senses did you enjoy reading about on these pages? Colour the symbols.

One Snowy Night

One snowy night,
I could see brown leaves on the ground.
One snowy night,
I could touch a soft snowflake.
One snowy night,
I could smell the burning hot fire.
One snowy night,
I could taste the wet snow falling in my mouth.

Belle Jackson (5)
St James' CE Primary School, St. Helens

On A Snowy Winter's Day

On a snowy winter's day,
I can see spiky snowflakes falling from the sky.
On a snowy winter's day
I can touch an icy pond.
On a snowy winter's day
I can smell hot chocolate in my kitchen.
On a snowy winter's day
I can taste yummy jam.
On a snowy winter's day
I can hear birds tweeting in a big tree.

Thomas Mason (6)
St James' CE Primary School, St. Helens

What senses did you enjoy reading about on these pages? Colour the symbols.

73

When Snow Falls

When snow falls,
I can see ice.
I can touch snowflakes.
I can smell hot dogs.
I can taste hot chocolate.
I can hear squirrels.

Ryan Miller (5)
St James' CE Primary School, St. Helens

When The Snow Falls

When the snow falls
I can see white snow.
When the snow falls
I can touch bumpy trees.
When the snow falls,
I can smell hot chocolate.
When the snow falls
I can taste warm tea.
When the snow falls
I can hear jumping rabbits.

Jack Prescott (5)
St James' CE Primary School, St. Helens

What senses did you enjoy reading about on these pages? Colour the symbols.

When The Snow Falls

I can see ice
I can touch snowflakes
I can smell hot chocolate
I can taste hot dogs
I can hear birds tweeting.

Jorden James Sarbutts (5)
St James' CE Primary School, St. Helens

When The Snow Falls

When the snow falls
I can see melting snow.
When the snow falls
i can touch snowflakes.
When the snow falls
i can smell hot chocolate.
When the snow falls
I can taste marshmallows.
When the snow falls
i can hear birds chirping.

Natalie Shannon (6)
St James' CE Primary School, St. Helens

What senses did you enjoy reading about on these pages? Colour the symbols.

When The Snow Falls

When the snow falls
I can see snowmen
I can touch snowballs
I can smell fire
I can taste warm milk
I can hear owls hooting.

Katie Shereen Tabern (5)
St James' CE Primary School, St. Helens

When The Snow Falls

When the snow falls
I can see pointy snowflakes.
When the snow falls
I can touch cold snow.
When the snow falls
I can smell hot chocolate.
When the snow falls
I can taste chips.
When the snow falls
I can hear jumping rabbits.

Ruby Warner-Southworth (6)
St James' CE Primary School, St. Helens

What senses did you enjoy reading about on these pages? Colour the symbols.

In The Dark, Dark Woods

In the dark, dark woods
I see a wolf
I hear wolves howling
I taste smoke
I touch flowers
I smell flowers.

Orla Callaghan (5)
St John Ogilvie Primary School, Paisley

In The Dark, Dark Woods

In the dark, dark woods
I see a fox
I smell foxes
I hear foxes barking
I taste apples
I touch apples
I smell apples
And I am not afraid
In the dark, dark woods.

Tyler Bourke (6)
St John Ogilvie Primary School, Paisley

What senses did you enjoy reading about on these pages? Colour the symbols.

In The Dark, Dark Woods

In the dark, dark woods
I see lightning
I hear howling
I taste smoke
I touch fur
I smell flowers.

Skye McGuire (5)
St John Ogilvie Primary School, Paisley

In The Dark, Dark Woods

In the dark, dark woods
I see bats flying above my head
I hear owls
I taste berries
I touch cats
I smell witches' nail varnish.

Freya Martin (5)
St John Ogilvie Primary School, Paisley

What senses did you enjoy reading about on these pages? Colour the symbols.

In The Dark, Dark Woods

In the dark, dark woods
I see bats flying
I hear owls *twit-twoo!*
I taste my saliva
I touch spiders
I smell skunks.

Emma Lynch (5)
St John Ogilvie Primary School, Paisley

In The Dark, Dark Woods

In the dark, dark woods
I see a wolf
I hear owls, *twit twoo!*
I taste my saliva
I touch feathers
I smell skunks.

Rory Price (5)
St John Ogilvie Primary School, Paisley

What senses did you enjoy reading about on these pages? Colour the symbols.

79

In The Dark, Dark Woods

In the dark, dark woods
I see bats flying in the sky
I hear bats squeaking
I taste dusty bats
I touch bats' wings
I smell bats' poo!

Jack Gibali (6)
St John Ogilvie Primary School, Paisley

In The Dark, Dark Woods

In the dark, dark woods
I see a wolf
I hear owls hooting
I taste green grass
I touch spiders
I smell gas.

Sean Chitsaka (6)
St John Ogilvie Primary School, Paisley

What senses did you enjoy reading about on these pages? Colour the symbols.

80

In The Dark, Dark Woods

In the dark, dark woods
I see a wolf
I hear footsteps
I taste my saliva
I touch foxes
I smell gas.

Harris Hunter (6)
St John Ogilvie Primary School, Paisley

In The Dark, Dark Woods

In the dark, dark woods
I see thunder and lighting
I hear bats squeaking
I taste apples
I touch cats
I smell witches' nail varnish.

Maria McIntyre (6)
St John Ogilvie Primary School, Paisley

What senses did you enjoy reading about on these pages? Colour the symbols.

In The Dark, Dark Woods

In the dark, dark woods
I see bats
I hear owls, *twit-twoo!*
I taste strawberries
I touch cats
I smell fire.

Ava Proctor (6)
St John Ogilvie Primary School, Paisley

In The Dark, Dark Woods

In the dark, dark woods
I see bats flying
I hear bats squeaking
I taste dusty bat
I touch bats' skin
I smell bats' poo!

Lukasz Lausz (6)
St John Ogilvie Primary School, Paisley

What senses did you enjoy reading about on these pages? Colour the symbols.

In The Dark, Dark Woods

In the dark, dark woods
I see a wolf
I hear owls, *twit twoo!*
I taste my saliva
I touch trees
I smell skunks.

Julian Scott (6)
St John Ogilvie Primary School, Paisley

In The Dark, Dark Woods

In the dark, dark woods
I see a wolf
I hear foxes barking
I taste apples
I touch foxes
I smell gas.

Daisy Jones (5)
St John Ogilvie Primary School, Paisley

What senses did you enjoy reading about on these pages? Colour the symbols.

83

In The Dark, Dark Woods

In the dark, dark woods
I see a fox
I hear owls, *twit twoo!*
I taste apples
I touch flowers petals
I smell flowers.

Emily Beattie (6)
St John Ogilvie Primary School, Paisley

In The Dark, Dark Woods

In the dark, dark woods
I see a fox
I hear foxes barking
I taste apples
I touch jaggy nettles
I smell apples.

Alexander Perry (6)
St John Ogilvie Primary School, Paisley

What senses did you enjoy reading about on these pages? Colour the symbols.

In The Dark, Dark Woods

In the dark, dark woods
I see thunder and lightning
I hear footsteps
I taste my saliva
I touch flowers
I smell smoke.

Charlotte Rush (5)
St John Ogilvie Primary School, Paisley

In The Dark, Dark Woods

In the dark, dark woods
I see bats and a wolf
I hear werewolves howling
I taste dusty bats
I touch werewolves' fur
I smell werewolves' poo!

Louis Wake (6)
St John Ogilvie Primary School, Paisley

What senses did you enjoy reading about on these pages? Colour the symbols.

In The Dark, Dark Woods

In the dark, dark woods
I see big trees
I hear owls hooting
I taste berries
I touch leaves
I smell smoke.

Ava Lina Smith (5)
St John Ogilvie Primary School, Paisley

Happiness

Happiness smells like my dog after it has been washed.
Happiness looks like a family out on their bikes on a sunny day.
Happiness sounds like my dog barking.
Happiness feels like the touch of my dog's fur.
Happiness tastes like a hot dog with ketchup.

Amelia Michalska (7)
St Patrick's Primary School, Portrush

What senses did you enjoy reading about on these pages? Colour the symbols.

Happiness

Happiness smells like chips
Happiness looks like children
Happiness sounds like musical instruments
Happiness feels like a soft blanket
Happiness tastes like Maltesers melting in my mouth.

Thomas Boorman (7)
St Patrick's Primary School, Portrush

Happiness

Happiness smells like new spring flowers
Happiness looks like my family
Happiness sounds like newborn lambs in the field
Happiness feels like my mummy's hugs
Happiness tastes like warm toast with jam.

Beatrice Byrne (7)
St Patrick's Primary School, Portrush

What senses did you enjoy reading about on these pages? Colour the symbols.

Happiness

Happiness smells like baby powder
Happiness looks like people smiling
Happiness sounds like the waves
Happiness feels like the warm sun
Happiness tastes like chocolate.

Jessica Quinn (7)
St Patrick's Primary School, Portrush

Happiness

Happiness smells like hot chocolate with marshmallows cooking on the stove
Happiness looks like my dogs going out on a walk
Happiness sounds like the sound of my dog licking me
Happiness feels like the touch of my dog's fur in my hands
Happiness tastes like Maltesers melting in my mouth.

Logan Mullan (7)
St Patrick's Primary School, Portrush

What senses did you enjoy reading about on these pages? Colour the symbols.

Happiness

Happiness smells like chocolate melting on a hot stove. Yum!
Happiness looks like my mum and dad kissing. *Ooh la la*!
Happiness sounds like the bell at 3 o'clock. Don't tell the teacher, yay!
Happiness feels like the touch of a football at my feet. Goal!
Happiness tastes like melted butter on toast. Meltastic!

John Mitchell (7)
St Patrick's Primary School, Portrush

Happiness

Happiness smells like sausages on the stove.
Happiness tastes like ice cream with a chocolate flake and mint sauce.
Happiness sounds like children cheering in the playground.
Happiness feels like silk on my skin.
Happiness looks like children smiling.

Jude Dallat (8)
St Patrick's Primary School, Portrush

What senses did you enjoy reading about on these pages? Colour the symbols.

Happiness

Happiness smells like sausages sizzling on a hot barbecue.
Happiness looks like my family on a day out.
Happiness sounds like the noise of Daddy doing something fun.
Happiness feels like hugs from my daddy.
Happiness tastes like warm toast with jam.

Tierna Smith (8)
St Patrick's Primary School, Portrush

Happiness

Happiness smells like smoke from my scrambler.
Happiness looks like my scrambler just before I get to ride it.
Happiness sounds like newborn chicks saying *cheep!*
Happiness feels like the touch of my dog's fur.
Happiness tastes like hot, spicy, pepperoni pizza.

Rory Dillon (7)
St Patrick's Primary School, Portrush

What senses did you enjoy reading about on these pages? Colour the symbols.

Happiness

Happiness smells like freshly cut grass.
Happiness looks like Jaidan and me playing football.
Happiness sounds like music.
Happiness feels like my teddy's fur as I cuddle him.
Happiness tastes like sweet honey on my tongue.

Luca McGowan (7)
St Patrick's Primary School, Portrush

Me

I can smell grass.
I can see Mrs McCavera.
I can hear talking.
I can feel glue.
I can taste sweets.

Dylan Williams (7)
St Patrick's Primary School, Portrush

What senses did you enjoy reading about on these pages? Colour the symbols.

Happiness

Happiness smells like chips bubbling in the frying pan.
Happiness looks like my dad playing football.
Happiness sounds like music.
Happiness feels like the touch of an ice cream cone in my hand.
Happiness tastes like chips and gravy.

Jaidan Patterson (7)
St Patrick's Primary School, Portrush

Happiness

Happiness smells like freshly cut grass
Happiness looks like me seeing my daddy
Happiness sounds like waves
Happiness feels like my puppy's fur
Happiness tastes like Oreos and warm milk.

Kyla Megan Hassan (6)
St Patrick's Primary School, Portrush

What senses did you enjoy reading about on these pages? Colour the symbols.

Happiness

Happiness smells like sweet candyfloss
Happiness looks like the sea sparkling in the sun
Happiness sounds like music in my ear
Happiness tastes like pancakes, my dear
Happiness feels complete when you are near

Charlie Shaw (7)
St Patrick's Primary School, Portrush

Happiness

Happiness looks like a lovely sky.
Happiness sounds like the lovely summer sea.
Happiness feels like a football at my feet.
Happiness tastes like sweet pancakes.

Eoin John Duggan (7)
St Patrick's Primary School, Portrush

What senses did you enjoy reading about on these pages? Colour the symbols.

Playground

In the trees I see bees, they sting me and that's how I feel
I smell the nice aroma of cookies on my plate
I can taste the small strawberries sliding in my mouth
I hear the buzzing bees fluttering around.

Matthew Inije (7)
St Paul's RC Primary School, Portsmouth

Playground

P eople running
L ike crazy, banging on the floor
A round you can see people
Y ucky
G irls around
R unning around
O utside you can see trees
U p in the air you can see birds
N ever go outside when it's raining, don't go out
D uring break you can have a snack.

Samuel Elms (7)
St Paul's RC Primary School, Portsmouth

What senses did you enjoy reading about on these pages? Colour the symbols.

Untitled

In the trees I see bees,
They sting me and that's how I feel
I smell the nice smell of cookies on my plate
I can taste the small strawberries sliding in my mouth
I hear the buzzing bees fluttering around.

Neema Saji (6)
St Paul's RC Primary School, Portsmouth

The Sun

The sun smells like lemonade
Which sparkles in the sunlight
I can feel smooth sand that sparkles in the sunlight
I can hear shouting children everywhere
I can taste twirly candy
I can see popcorn that looks poppy.

Jimnah George (6)
St Paul's RC Primary School, Portsmouth

What senses did you enjoy reading about on these pages? Colour the symbols.

Autumn

Hot chocolate
Fluffy rabbits
Nice ice cream
Leaves falling
It's cold.

Patrick Carsey (6)
South Hill Primary School, Hemel Hempstead

Autumn

Fireworks crackle
Roast dinners
Woolly hat
Cuddly squirrels
Leaves falling down
Squirrels burying nuts.

Jamie Benjamin Wells (5)
South Hill Primary School, Hemel Hempstead

What senses did you enjoy reading about on these pages? Colour the symbols.

Autumn

Blanket of leaves
Shiny fireworks
Leaves falling on my head
Warm hot chocolate
Throwing leaves.

Oliver Davies-Moon (5)
South Hill Primary School, Hemel Hempstead

Autumn

Leaves falling
Acorns coming out
Hot chocolate
I played in the trees.

Finley Talbot (5)
South Hill Primary School, Hemel Hempstead

What senses did you enjoy reading about on these pages? Colour the symbols.

Autumn

Leaves falling on the ground
Very soft robins
Blanket of leaves
Yummy hot chocolate.

Ryan Blake Schofield (5)
South Hill Primary School, Hemel Hempstead

Autumn

Wet rain
Fireworks
Wet puddles
Hot mug
Red leaves
Crunchy leaves
Lots of squirrels and acorns
Roast potatoes.

Isla Stobie (5)
South Hill Primary School, Hemel Hempstead

What senses did you enjoy reading about on these pages? Colour the symbols.

Autumn

I see red leaves
I hear squirrels eating acorns
I smell hot chocolate
I taste woods
I feel squishy mud.

Aaima Ayesha Islam (5)
South Hill Primary School, Hemel Hempstead

Autumn

I see red leaves
I hear fireworks
I smell the mist
I taste nutmeg
I feel leaves on my head.

Joely Burrows (5)
South Hill Primary School, Hemel Hempstead

What senses did you enjoy reading about on these pages? Colour the symbols.

Autumn

I see yellow leaves
I hear wind
I smell bonfires
I taste hot chocolate
I feel warm.

Brooke Barnes (5)
South Hill Primary School, Hemel Hempstead

Autumn

I see red-brown leaves
I hear creatures
I smell fireworks
I taste hot chocolate
I feel nice leaves.

Caelan Jacob Bruce (5)
South Hill Primary School, Hemel Hempstead

What senses did you enjoy reading about on these pages? Colour the symbols.

Autumn

Leaves falling
Empty branches
A squirrel hibernating
Glistening leaves falling.

Tanya Knight (5)
South Hill Primary School, Hemel Hempstead

Autumn

I taste chocolate
Birds flying from the tree
I play in the leaves
I like to touch branches
I see a squirrel.

Hudson Harte (6)
South Hill Primary School, Hemel Hempstead

What senses did you enjoy reading about on these pages? Colour the symbols.

Autumn

I see leaves falling
I hear wind blowing
I smell a bonfire
I taste hot roast
I feel squishy mud.

Callum Jell (6)
South Hill Primary School, Hemel Hempstead

Autumn

I see squirrels hibernating
I hear leaves falling from the trees.

Ashlee Nicole Jones (6)
South Hill Primary School, Hemel Hempstead

What senses did you enjoy reading about on these pages? Colour the symbols.

Autumn

I see leaves cover the ground
I hear crunchy leaves
I smell foggy days
I taste hot chocolate
I feel cold.

Japneet Singh (5)
South Hill Primary School, Hemel Hempstead

Autumn

I see autumn
I hear leaves crunching
I smell wet rain
I taste apples
I feel cold wind.

James Dawes (6)
South Hill Primary School, Hemel Hempstead

What senses did you enjoy reading about on these pages? Colour the symbols.

103

Autumn

I like hot chocolate
I hear birds sing
I like sweets
I like to touch crunchy leaves
A blanket of leaves on the playground.

Ronnie Tilson (6)
South Hill Primary School, Hemel Hempstead

Autumn

Hot chocolate
Swooshy wind
A squirrel hibernating
Roast dinner
Red leaves are falling
Warm, hot blanket.

Freya Allford (5)
South Hill Primary School, Hemel Hempstead

What senses did you enjoy reading about on these pages? Colour the symbols.

Autumn

I see acorns
I hear leaves crunch
I smell wind
I taste cool air
I feel hot chocolate.

Sophie Harrington (5)
South Hill Primary School, Hemel Hempstead

Autumn

Some red leaves are falling
Some breaking branches are creaking
Some hot chocolate is my favourite
Some fireworks are bright.

Zara Nield (5)
South Hill Primary School, Hemel Hempstead

What senses did you enjoy reading about on these pages? Colour the symbols.

Autumn

Leaves falling
It was foggy
The trees are turning red
It is turning colder
A blanket of leaves
Crunchy leaves.

Rory Stewart (5)
South Hill Primary School, Hemel Hempstead

Autumn

Leaves falling down
Birds tweeting
Hot chocolate
Warm hot potato
Fireworks banging
Red leaves.

Kiena McFarlane (6)
South Hill Primary School, Hemel Hempstead

What senses did you enjoy reading about on these pages? Colour the symbols.

Dragon Fruit

It looks red and prickly like a dragon's tail
It feels smooth and soft with sharp spikes all around it
It tastes like a carrot but squishy and wet
It smells funny and waxy and wet.

Emma Brookes (6)
The Cobbs Infant School, Warrington

Fruit

F resh, red strawberries growing on the trees
R osy ripe apples, round like a ball
U nderneath the skin there is a juicy, fleshy middle
I nside watery juice squirts out
T reat yourself to a soft banana.

Bella May Ratcliffe (6)
The Cobbs Infant School, Warrington

What senses did you enjoy reading about on these pages? Colour the symbols.

Chocolate

I can hear the hard chocolate bar in my mouth
As hard as a stone.
I can feel the lovely chocolate bar melting in my hand
As watery as water
I can taste the amazing chocolate bar in my mouth
As lovely as you.

Mia Warren (6)
Woodlands Primary School, Borehamwood

(White) Chocolate

Chocolate, chocolate,
You are my friend
You are as white as wallpaper,
Yum, yum, yum.

Chocolate, chocolate,
You are my friend
The smell of melted chocolate
Mmm, mmm, mmm.

Chocolate, chocolate
You are my friend.

Joel Barrass (6)
Woodlands Primary School, Borehamwood

What senses did you enjoy reading about on these pages? Colour the symbols.

Chocolate

Chocolate, chocolate
You are my favourite sweet
I love you so much
Chocolate, chocolate
You are fabulous stuff
I love you with all my heart
Chocolate, chocolate
You are my wonderful friend
I won't forget you.

Youlin Huang (6)
Woodlands Primary School, Borehamwood

What senses did you enjoy reading about on these pages? Colour the symbols.

Young Writers Information

We hope you have enjoyed reading this book – and that you will continue to in the coming years.

If you're a young writer who enjoys reading and creative writing, or the parent of an enthusiastic poet or story writer, do visit our website **www.youngwriters.co.uk**. Here you will find free competitions, workshops and games, as well as recommended reads, a poetry glossary and our blog.

If you would like to order further copies of this book, or any of our other titles give us a call or visit **www.youngwriters.co.uk**.

Young Writers
Remus House
Coltsfoot Drive
Peterborough
PE2 9BF

(01733) 890066
info@youngwriters.co.uk

Share your feelings verse any time!